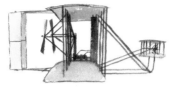

Table of Contents

Flying a Kite, 1899   1

Bumpy Rides, 1900-1901   10

Twists and Turns, 1901-1902   22

Props and Power, 1902-1903   28

The Wright Flyer, 1903   34

Onward and Upward   41

Taking Flight

THE STORY OF THE WRIGHT BROTHERS

Written by
Stephen Krensky

Illustrated by
Larry Day

Ready-to-Read
Aladdin Paperbacks

For my father—
one of the original frequent fliers

First Aladdin Paperbacks edition May 2001

Text copyright © 2000 by Stephen Krensky
Illustrations copyright © 2000 by Larry Day

Aladdin Paperbacks
An imprint of Simon & Schuster Children's Publishing Division
1230 Avenue of the Americas
New York, NY 10020

The text for this book was set in Utopia.
The illustrations were rendered in watercolor.
Printed and bound in the United States of America
2 4 6 8 10 9 7 5 3 1

The Library of Congress has cataloged the hardcover edition as follows:
Krensky, Stephen.
Taking flight : the story of the Wright brothers / by Stephen Krensky ;
illustrated by Larry Day.
p.   cm. (Ready-to-read)
Summary: Describes how the Wright Brothers came
to build and fly the first powered aircraft.
ISBN: 0-689-81225-6 (hc.)
[1. Wright, Wilbur, 1867-1912—Juvenile literature.
2. Wright, Orville, 1871–1948—Juvenile literature.
3. Aeronautics—United States—Biography—Juvenile literature.
4. Wright, Orville, 1871–1948. 5. Wright, Wilbur, 1867–1912.
6. Aeronautics—Biography.]
I. Day, Larry, ill. II. Title. III. Series.
TL540.W7K74   2000
629.13/0092/2   [B]—21
98-34712   AC
ISBN: 0-689-81224-8 (Aladdin pbk.)

Flying a Kite
1899

The cloth-covered kite looked like a very strange bird. It rose and fell on the wind, turning with each new breeze. But this was not a small bird. It had two five-foot wings, one set above the other.

From the ground below, a balding thirty-two-year-old man controlled the glider like an upside-down puppet. His name was Wilbur Wright.

Cords ran from the glider's wings to crossed sticks in Wilbur's hands. When he pulled the sticks down to the left, the glider's left wing tip twisted—and the glider curved to the left. If he pulled the sticks down to the right, the glider's right wing tip twisted—and the glider curved to the right.

Wilbur and his brother Orville had built the glider in nearby Dayton, Ohio. There they had a shop where they built and sold bicycles. They liked to use their hands to tinker with a printing press or build a new porch for the house they shared with their father and sister.

The Wrights had been interested in flying objects for a long time. In 1878, when Wilbur was eleven and Orville just seven, their father had given them a surprise. "Father brought home to us a small toy actuated by a rubber spring," Orville later wrote, "which would lift itself into the air." This little helicopter—made of bamboo, paper, and cork—excited both boys. Soon they were building their own small flying machines.

The Wrights carried into adulthood their dream of flying, but such dreams were not new. The subject of flight had been popular since ancient times. In one Greek myth, the architect Daedelus made two sets of wings from feathers and wax. He and his son, Icarus, used them to fly across the sea. The wings worked until Icarus flew too close to the sun. When the sun's heat melted the wax, Icarus fell into the sea and drowned.

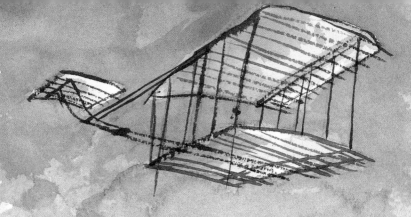

Fortunately, Orville and Wilbur weren't working with wax and feathers, but with a glider made of wood. When Wilbur met Orville after testing the kite, he told his brother that they were on the right track. It was possible to control a glider's flight by twisting or warping its wings.

This kind of control was important. The Wrights worried, after all, about what would happen after the aircraft was aloft. They had no interest in hot-air balloons, which only drifted on the wind. The Wrights wanted to steer their own way through the air.

Orville was pleased by Wilbur's report, but not surprised. He and Wilbur had thought long and hard before building the glider, as they did about almost everything. They worked together, ate together, and sometimes finished each other's sentences. Wilbur was quieter than Orville—who had a mustache and wore fancier clothes— but the two brothers were closer than twins.

They had already read the few books about flying machines they could find. They also had begun to study birds in flight. The wing-warping was a test of what they had learned so far.

Wilbur wrote to his father, who was

away from home, that he was exploring the subject ". . . for pleasure rather than profit." That was wise, because the birds made flying look far easier than it really was.

Bumpy Rides
1900–1901

Flying was dangerous. As Wilbur and Orville knew, several men had been hurt or killed in earlier experiments. The Wrights were eager to fly, but they also wanted to survive the process.

Their next step was to build a glider big enough to hold a man—and see if they could control it from the air or the ground. The *No. 1*, as they named it, had a wooden framework, support wires, and fine sateen fabric covering the seventeen-foot wingspan. It also featured a stick called a front elevator, or horizontal rudder, which controlled upward or downward motion.

The glider's wings were curved, reflecting the work of the British inventor Sir George Cayley. In the early 1800s, Cayley had noticed that birds fly with their wings curved, not flat. He thought that man-made wings should follow the birds' example. His experiments showed that during flight, air did not pass the same way above and below a curved wing.

Below the wing, Cayley discovered, the air traveled in a straight line. But above the wing, the air followed the wing's bulging curve—a longer distance. The air above the wing had to move faster to keep up with the air passing below the wing.

Faster-moving air does not crowd in one place as much as slower-moving air. Its pressure is lower. So under a curved wing, the slower-moving air, being crowded, pushes toward the more open space above it. This upward push, or lift, makes the wing rise.

Cayley's ideas were ignored because most scientists of his time simply thought manned flight was impossible. Still, he continued to work. In 1853, one of his gliders went a short way carrying his coachman—who found the ride so upsetting that he quit on the spot.

To test their glider, the Wrights needed very strong winds to lift the curved wings. The closest place they could find was a village called Kitty Hawk, on the North Carolina coast. Kitty Hawk had sandy beaches where the glider could land—or crash—gently.

Fishing was the only business in Kitty Hawk. So the arrival of two men in store-bought suits and starched collars caused a bit of a stir. The citizens of Kitty Hawk were not impressed, though. They shared the popular opinion that people were not meant to fly.

The Wrights called their trip a vacation, but it was hardly restful. They cooked their own meals and camped in tents on the beach. Supplies arrived on a once-a-week ferry. Some nights, Orville wrote to his sister, Katharine, "the wind shaking the roof and sides of the tent sounds exactly like thunder . . . the sand fairly blinds us . . . We certainly can't complain of the place. We came down here for wind and sand, and we have got them."

At first the high winds forced the Wrights to fly the glider as a kite, with no one on board. On later flights, one brother would lie on top of the glider's body, or fuselage, while the other held the wing and ran downhill into the wind until the glider took off. Their longest glide lasted twenty seconds and covered perhaps four hundred feet.

After a month, the brothers went home, but they returned again the next July. They set up camp four miles away from Kitty Hawk, at Kill Devil Hills. On this visit they had two assistants. Some days, mosquitoes seemed to cover everything. As Orville wrote: "They chewed us clear through our underwear and socks."

Still, the four men set to work. This year's glider, the *No. 2*, had legs like skis, for takeoffs along a wooden track. It also had a twenty-two-foot wingspan.

With the *No. 2*, the pilot had more control over the wing-warping than before. The *No. 1* had used awkward foot controls. The *No. 2* had a hip cradle—a harness for the pilot to slip into. Cables connected the harness to the wings. As the pilot twisted his hips to one side, the harness moved the cables and warped the wings.

Day after day, the Wright brothers dragged their glider to a sandy hilltop. Though their longest glide improved on the year before, neither Wilbur nor Orville could claim real control of the glider, and both had accidents. After six tiring weeks of tinkering, it was clear that only the mosquitoes were enjoying themselves.

In August, the Wrights packed up and returned home. Wilbur still believed that one day man would fly. He just wasn't sure it would happen in his lifetime.

Twists and Turns
1901–1902

Although 1901 saw the first mass-produced American cars take to the road, a real flying machine still seemed very far away. One expert said that the first airships would be built soon, but they would be only big enough to carry a bug.

Wilbur and Orville knew better than to listen to such talk. Over the winter of 1901–1902, they built a six-foot wind tunnel. This long, wooden box had a fan at one end and a window in the top. The Wrights tested dozens of small metal wings to see which shapes worked best in the tunnel.

The Wrights' careful approach was unusual. Few people realized that gliding was a science. Some just attached birdlike wings to their backs, jumped from a high place, and hoped for the best.

One man who shared the Wrights' approach was Otto Lilienthal. This German airman had begun flying in 1891. Over the next five years he made over 2,000 glides. In the air, Lilienthal swung his body to steer his hanging glider in different directions. One day a strong wind sent him crashing to the ground. The fall broke his back, and he died a few hours later.

The Wrights knew what had happened to Lilienthal, and they were careful. As Wilbur later stated, anyone who wanted to solve a problem "must not take dangerous risks."

The Wrights returned to Kill Devil Hills in August of 1902 with a new glider, their third, packed in crates. By mid-September they had put it together. Once again the wingspan had grown—it was now thirty-two feet. They also gave the glider a vertical tail to make it more stable.

The biggest change was in the wing-warping controls. These were now connected to the tail fin so both could be moved at the same time. This let the pilot adjust the glider's balance more quickly and safely.

Dragging the heavy glider through the sand was hard work, so the Wrights tried to learn something from every glide and avoid crash landings. They made almost a thousand glides that fall. In the most successful glide, the glider rose thirty feet in the air while traveling more than five hundred feet along the ground.

When Wilbur and Orville returned home in October, they had solved most of their control and steering problems. Their glider might not be perfect, but it worked. Nobody else in the world could say that.

Props and Power
1902–1903

The Wright brothers were pleased by their progress, but they weren't done yet. To fly without wind, the glider would need its own source of power. Then it would be a true flying machine.

Other people had used engines to turn propellers in boats. As Wilbur and Orville had once seen with their toy helicopter, propellers could also be used in the air. In fact, the Italian painter and scientist Leonardo da Vinci was the first to think of using propellers to lift people off the ground. He had sketched the plan for such a machine four hundred years earlier.

In 1902, though, very little was known about propeller design. Propellers work like fans. As the blades turn, they push the air behind them. This makes the propeller go forward. If the propeller is attached to a glider, that glider goes forward, too.

But what shape should propellers be to move a flying machine? Some inventors favored the same shape used in boats. The Wrights did not agree. Water and air were not the same—even though they were both affected by things moving through them.

Wilbur and Orville tested many propeller shapes in their wind tunnel that winter. Finally they designed and built a pair of propellers eight and one-eighth feet long. They were made from three layers of spruce wood carefully glued together and shaped with hand tools. "Well," Orville wrote to a friend, "our propellers are so different from any that have been used before that they will have to be either a good deal better, or a good deal worse."

Power for the propellers was also a problem. Steam engines had been tried in the past. The engines alone were not too heavy, but they did not work by themselves. They needed steam-making boilers—filled with water—to run, which added added too much weight to the flying machine.

The Wrights were not the only people working on this problem. Samuel Langley, the head of the Smithsonian Institution, had been building flying machines as well. Langley had catapulted glider models with fourteen-foot wingspans into the air—and one had flown for half a mile.

Langley worked with an engine that used a new fuel called gasoline. But the gas engine used in the new automobiles was too heavy for the glider to lift.

So Wilbur and Orville rolled up their sleeves and went to work. With the help

of Charlie Taylor, a mechanic who worked in their bicycle shop, they made their own twelve-horsepower gasoline engine. It weighed about 140 pounds, sixty pounds less than any similar engine.

Wilbur and Orville thought they now had all the pieces of their puzzle. The time had come to put the pieces together and see if they fit.

The Wright Flyer
1903

As Wilbur and Orville prepared to test their flying machine, the newspapers reported that a car had made the first trip across the country—in sixty-three days. The Wrights may not have known this. They were still trying to get their flying machine off the ground.

They had been working on their new aircraft—*The Wright Flyer*—since returning to Kill Devil Hills in late September. Bad storms and freezing weather slowed their progress. The Wrights measured the cold by counting the items they used to keep warm. Wilbur wrote home that they were used to "5 blanket nights." But when it got really cold, they used "5 blankets, 2 quilts and a fire."

Despite their careful planning, the Wrights still had problems. In November, the propeller shafts developed cracks, forcing Orville back to Dayton to have new ones made. On his return, he read that Samuel Langley's full-sized aircraft, which he called an aerodrome, had crashed upon takeoff.

Despite this news, the Wrights had faith in their skills and equipment. The *Flyer* had a longer forty-foot wingspan, but the biggest change, of course, was the addition of the engine and two propellers. These were mounted between the two wings, behind the pilot's feet.

With the weather getting worse, the Wrights tried a flight on December 15. They both dressed formally in dark suits. Wilbur won a coin toss to see who would fly first. But the *Flyer* rose too sharply at takeoff. The engine stalled, and the 605-pound *Flyer* crashed into the sand.

It took two days to repair the *Flyer.* December 17 dawned cold and windy. Orville and Wilbur waited a couple of hours, hoping the weather would improve. It didn't.

For once the Wrights were too impatient to wait any longer. As the two brothers shook hands, one onlooker noticed that they looked "like two folks parting who weren't sure they'd ever see one another again."

Now it was Orville's turn to fly. He

stretched out on the fuselage, grasping the controls. As the flying machine started to move, Wilbur ran alongside, steadying the wing. Against a head-wind, the glider gained speed slowly. Once in the air, it jerked up and down like a bucking bronco.

The flight lasted just twelve seconds, and the aircraft was never more than ten feet off the ground. The distance crossed—120 feet—was no more than a good stone's throw.

But history had been made. As Orville wrote, the flight was the first "in which a machine carrying a man had raised itself by its own power into the air in full flight, had sailed forward without reduction of speed, and had finally landed at a point as high as that from which it had started."

Onward and Upward

Within ten months, Orville and Wilbur were taking twenty-four-mile flights lasting almost forty minutes. Several years passed before anyone else matched this level of aerial control. The gap shows how clearly the Wrights led the way in building and flying the first airplanes.

By 1910 new airplanes—many designed or inspired by the Wrights—were breaking records for speed and flight. Passengers were first carried on a twenty-two-mile flight between Tampa and St. Petersburg, Florida, in 1914. The first non-stop flight across the country came in 1923. And in 1927 Charles Lindbergh was the first man to fly solo across the Atlantic Ocean.

Wilbur Wright missed these advances, having died of typhoid fever in 1912. Orville, however, lived until 1948. It was the dawn of the jet age, and he had been retired for many years. But no one ever forgot that he and Wilbur had been the first to take flight, leading the way where only the birds had gone before.

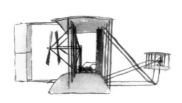